ANOTHER WAY OF LOOKING

HELPING YOU CHALLENGE THE ASSUMPTIONS OF TODAY'S CULTURE

JOHN DE WIT

Foreword by
Lesslie Newbigin

D1347631

BIBLE SOCIETY
Stonehill Green, Westlea, Swindon, Wilts SN5 7DG

© John de Wit 1990

All rights reserved. No part of this publication may be reproduced, stored in a retrieval system, or transmitted, in any form or by any means, electronic, mechanical, photocopying, recording or otherwise without the prior permission of The British and Foreign Bible Society.

Unless otherwise stated, quotations from the Bible are from the Good News Bible, published by the Bible Societies/Collins, © American Bible Society, New York, 1966, 1971, 1976.

ISBN 0 564 05875 0

Printed in Great Britain by Tekprint Ltd, Swindon

Bible Societies exist to provide resources for Bible distribution and use. Bible Society in England and Wales (BFBS) is a member of the United Bible Societies, an international partnership working in over 180 countries. Their common aim is to reach all people with the Bible, or some part of it, in a language they can understand and at a price they can afford. Parts of the Bible have now been translated into approximately 1900 languages. Bible Societies aim to help every church at every point where it uses the Bible. You are invited to share in this work by your prayers and gifts. Bible Society in your country will be very happy to provide details of its activity.

ACKNOWLEDGEMENT

This study guide began life as part of a course run by St George's House, Windsor. Their part in its development is gratefully acknowledged.

CONTENTS

FOREWORD

The Apostle Paul tells his readers that their surrender to Christ must include the renewing of their minds (Romans 12.2). As we prepare for the Decade of Evangelism and consider what is involved in the calling of all people to the allegiance of Christ, it is necessary to recognize how far the assumptions which govern our public life are alien to the mind shaped by Christian faith. In this series of studies John de Wit has provided a way in which, as members of Christian congregations, we may test our unexamined assumptions in the light of the gospel. The exercises have been tested in use and refined. Through the good offices of Bible Society they are now made available to all who can profit by their use. I am very grateful both to John de Wit and to Bible Society, and I hope and pray that this small publication may help many people towards that renewing of the mind for which the Apostle called.

Lesslie Newbigin

Introduction

Is God No Longer Needed?

People don't bother about church as much as they used to. Most people seem to get on with life without needing or caring about religion. Some are hostile to the Church, but more are simply indifferent.

Christianity is no longer the force it once was in Western Europe. People once talked of "Christendom": it was a time when nearly everyone was a Christian (of sorts), and when the churches were full. That Christendom is a thing of the past.

The churches are only too ready to blame themselves for their decline. Better clergy, more committed laity, more exciting worship, brighter hymns, better translations are all attempts to reverse the trend. In their battle to survive, some churches lose heart. Others close ranks and deaden the pain of society's indifference by becoming close-knit religious clubs. One thing is sure: the Church in Western Europe is back in a missionary situation. All Christians are going to have to learn how to explain their beliefs to their secular neighbours. We can no longer assume that most people "out there" know what Christianity is about.

But before we lose heart through self-imposed guilt and a sense of helplessness, we should remember the story of David and Goliath and look carefully around us. For the society in which Christianity used to rule has changed out of all recognition since the days of "Christendom". During much of the history of Western Europe, ordinary people had little or no say about anything. They lived under the authority of those in power, which included the Church, and such authority was seldom questioned. There was a time when kings and princes were held to be appointed by God and possessed awesome powers. Ordinary folk were extremely dependent on their "betters", whether this was the landowner or, more recently, the factory owner. Life for many was merely tough.

What immense changes there have been in the lot of ordinary people in the past hundred or so years. A series of industrial and technological revolutions has transformed the material quality of most ordinary people's lives. Political changes have created popular democracy, and social changes have destroyed the idea that people are born into a certain "station" in life and must remain there. Compulsory primary and secondary education for everyone encourages more people to think for themselves and to ask questions. Scientific discoveries have transformed our understanding of the universe. Add to that the recent enormous changes in transport and communication, and you begin to see what a changed world Christianity has had to keep pace with.

It is hardly surprising with such vast changes in society that there have been big changes in the way that people think. Old beliefs, attitudes and traditions have been challenged. People are less ready to accept things because they are told to accept them: they rightly question and probe everything. And they are free to believe, think, and say what they like. Inevitably the result is a variety of beliefs and attitudes: a pluralism that is very different from the single viewpoint of Christendom. These changes do not necessarily make Christian beliefs outdated. But Christians must resist the temptation to look back to a Christendom that will never return. Instead we should do two things.

Firstly, we should try to understand the beliefs and assumptions of the Western secular culture that we live in. This is not at all easy because we are in the middle of that culture ourselves and we often unwittingly share its assumptions. And yet, as we shall see later on, many of the attitudes, beliefs and assumptions of the secular culture in which we live are very different from the Christian standpoint. So our first task is to stop and listen, and to learn how our neighbours think about life and what makes them tick. Without doing this we shall never understand why they have difficulties in understanding what we believe.

The second thing that as ordinary Christians we should do is to learn how to present our faith so that other people will understand. We cannot just quote scripture without explaining what it means in simple, everyday language. Too often, the language we use to those outside the community of faith only means something to other Christians. It's the language of the Bible or theology books and it doesn't cut much ice in the secular world. Many of us are tongue-tied as Christians. We haven't learned how to put our deepest beliefs into simple words. We often feel very inadequate and afraid, and yet our Gospel message is a message that our modern secular culture urgently needs to hear. People in the 'nineties need to hear that at the heart of the universe there is not Nothing, but Love. They need to know that all our endeavours, however magnificent, are nothing without Love. They need to understand that the secular culture of the West is fatally flawed if it is based on self-interest, power and injustice. However invincible it seems today, it will go the way of every other empire if half the world is left in poverty and hunger. That is why the proclamation of God's Kingdom is as vital today as it was 2,000 years ago.

In the last few years a number of writers have begun to help Christians to see how the secular world thinks, and have tried to identify some of the assumptions on which modern Western culture is based. This short study course tries to follow their lead and look at a few popular assumptions from a Christian point of view. I hope the course will also help you to understand some of the stumbling blocks that prevent other people from accepting or even understanding Christianity. And I hope it will give my fellow Christians help and encouragement in presenting their faith to others.

HOW TO USE THIS COURSE

The following six sessions are designed to be used by Christian groups, although they could be used by individuals for personal Bible study. Each session tries to follow an argument, starting from a contemporary attitude or assumption and ending up with a Christian point of view based on a Bible study. In a group the argument before the first exercise could be read out by a member of the group. The exercise is intended to help the members of the group to understand the argument and should take about 20 minutes. After the exercise, a member of the group can continue to read the argument up to the Bible study passage. The passage can be read out and then the group can tackle the questions together, taking about 35–40 minutes over this. Finally, each member of the group should spend a few minutes filling in the "What would you say" exercise, and then share their thoughts with the rest of the group when everybody is ready. This might take another 20 minutes. Each of the six sessions will probably take about 1½ hours.

WHAT YOU WILL NEED BEFORE MEETING

Each member of the group should have a copy of this booklet, some paper and something to write with. In the first session every member of the group should bring a newspaper. Bibles will be helpful for the following sessions.

Before each meeting members of the group should read through the argument of the session they are going to do, to get themselves thinking.

A WORD TO GROUP LEADERS

It is quite difficult to get inside some of the ideas in this booklet. Group leaders will therefore need to be able to think

4

clearly so that they can help a group sort out fairly complicated ideas. On the other hand, a group leader should not be
so dominant that they impose their own ideas on the group,
or feed everyone the "right answers" when the group gets
stuck.

Group leaders should see themselves primarily as time-
keepers and chairpersons rather than as teachers. Your job is
to get the group started, keep them gently to the point, and
keep them to time.

You need also to spot quiet members and encourage them
to offer their opinions, and gently but firmly to make sure that
dominant and very talkative members are not allowed to hog
the floor. This can often be done by inviting other members of
the group to offer their opinion or to say whether they agree
or disagree with what is being said.

Group leaders should also try to spot red herrings and
group members' hobby horses, pointing out gently that these
are not what the discussion is about.

The best-run groups are not those where people talk a lot,
but those where people are really listening to each other, so
don't be afraid of silences when they occur.

Before each session, read the material through so that you
know what it's about, and what the group is supposed to be
doing during the meeting. But once the meeting starts
remember that you will be learning alongside everyone else—
so don't worry if you don't know all the answers. You are not
there to provide answers!

The best group work can only be done when people know
and begin to trust each other. It can be a good idea to set up an
introductory exercise at the first meeting. Ask people to
divide into pairs and discover from each other their names
and what they hope to gain from the course. Let them talk for
five minutes and then gather everyone together again, and
ask each person to introduce the person he or she was paired
with.

Finally, begin or end with prayer. After all, it is the Holy Spirit who is the Spirit of Truth and so helps us to look at things another way.

SESSION ONE

"Seeing is believing"

We live in a culture which emphasizes things that can be seen. Television, advertising, magazines, popular newspapers and displays in shops and offices depend more on pictures than on words. Advertisers spend millions on creating images for their customers: visual statements of ideas.

From a very early age people are taught to value objectivity. This also has to do with what you can see, touch, measure and analyse. Objectivity is the basis of the scientific approach: a way of thinking that is not emotional or subjective. It is also highly valued in most other areas of life. It is the basis of reason.

Things that can be established objectively are called facts. They are the bedrock of knowledge. You have to know your facts. Facts are nice, definite things: you either know them or you don't.

In contrast to facts are beliefs and values. These are slippery things and much more difficult to deal with. You can't see them, although you can analyse them and you can work out whether they are consistent with themselves—whether they "add up". Perhaps because beliefs and values are not easy to pin down, our culture tends not to give them prominence. The world of industry, commerce and science prefers to stick to facts and be as objective as it can. In reality, as we shall discuss in the next session, the whole of society is buzzing with beliefs and values of one kind or another. Officially, however, public life is conducted on the basis of "facts".

This particularly affects attitudes to religious beliefs. Our Western secular culture regards religious beliefs as having little to do with the objective world of facts. And so, for many people, religion is best kept out of public affairs. As you can't see God, or measure him or analyse him, belief in him is a private option, but not something that ought to come into public life. The result is that modern society divides life into a public world of facts and a private world of beliefs and values. God is kept out of council chamber or boardroom or work-place, and is confined to the private and domestic world of personal religion. God is there on Sundays for those who choose to worship him, but for most of the week in the "real" world of politics and economics and industry he is absent. Even Christians can claim to believe in and value God, but live their daily lives as practical atheists.

TO DO

Take any daily newspaper—a group might look at several different ones—and see how many times God is mentioned.

If you find that he is mentioned, what is the story about and what does it tell you about people's attitudes to belief in God?

If God is not mentioned, what is the significance of that?

Spend 15 minutes on this

When you start to think about beliefs and facts you discover that they can't be so neatly kept apart. Anyone who enjoys detective stories will know that clues are not just the things you can see with a magnifying glass. Hidden motives come into detective work too. Nobody looks at life in a totally objective way. We all have beliefs, attitudes, values and opinions which colour the way we look at things. We interpret the facts according to our beliefs and values all the time. So it's not only the things which you can see and touch and measure that are real. There is also a sometimes hidden world

8

of ideas, ideals, beliefs, values, feelings and opinions which is just as real and just as important in human affairs.

TO DO

Look at the newspapers again and take one or two controversial issues in the news.

What are the beliefs, values and feelings behind these issues?

Spend 15 minutes on this

So beliefs and values are often as important as facts. Which means that religious beliefs cannot simply be pushed to one side as unimportant. Religious beliefs *are* important however much some people would like to abolish them.

More importantly, the Christian faith is not a system of beliefs that has no relationship to the facts of everyday life. God cannot normally be seen or touched or measured like an object. There can never be scientific proof that he exists. But that does not mean that Christian beliefs about God have been plucked out of the air. Christians believe that God has made himself known to people during the course of history. We believe that he still makes himself known to people today. Above all, we believe that God made himself known in a unique way in the person of Jesus Christ. This conviction inspired John to write these famous words.

BIBLE STUDY

Before the world was created, the Word already existed; he was with God, and he was the same as God. From the very beginning the Word was with God. Through him God made all things; not one thing in all creation was made without him. The Word was the source of life, and this life brought light to mankind. The light shines in the darkness, and the darkness has never put it out.

God sent his messenger, a man named John, who came to tell people about the light, so that all should hear the message and believe. He himself was not the light; he came to

9

tell about the light. This was the real light—the light that comes into the world and shines on all mankind.

The Word was in the world, and though God made the world through him, yet the world did not recognize him. He came to his own country, but his own people did not receive him. Some, however, did receive him and believed in him; so he gave them the right to become God's children. They did not become God's children by natural means, that is, by being born as the children of a human father; God himself was their Father.

The Word became a human being and, full of grace and truth, lived among us. We saw his glory, the glory which he received as the Father's only Son.

John spoke about him. He cried out, "This is the one I was talking about when I said, 'He comes after me, but he is greater than I am, because he existed before I was born.'"

Out of the fullness of his grace he has blessed us all, giving us one blessing after another. God gave the Law through Moses, but grace and truth came through Jesus Christ. No one has ever seen God. The only Son, who is the same as God and is at the Father's side, he has made him known.

John 1.1–18

SOME QUESTIONS

1 How, from John's perspective, does God make himself known in history?

2 When God's Word became visible in human form, what were his characteristics and what effects did he have?

3 Why do you think that God chose to reveal himself as a person?

What would you say . . .
. . . to somebody who can't believe in God because he can't be seen?

10

SESSION TWO

"It doesn't matter what you believe as long as you're sincere"

If you asked half a dozen artists to paint a picture of the same landscape, you would get six different pictures. The basic features of the landscape, the trees, the buildings and the river would be the same. But each painting would look different, because each painter interprets the subject in a different way.

What is true for painters is true for all of us. Nobody ever looks at life in a purely objective way. We interpret what we see and hear. The basic facts of life may be the same, but we look at them in different ways. To some people, for example, a nuclear power station is a triumph of scientific and technological skill, while to others it is a hazard. The object in both cases is the same, but it is seen in different ways.

The way we look at life is influenced by our ideas, attitudes, beliefs and values. We use belief and value systems to make sense of our experience. They are what enable us to form an overall picture of life. If facts are like individual jigsaw pieces, belief and value systems are like the picture on the box that contains the jigsaw. Using the picture on the box, you can work out how all the jigsaw pieces fit together. Belief and value systems enable people to interpret the facts and fit them together into an overall picture.

Beliefs and values may constitute clearly definable systems such as religious beliefs, or philosophical or political ideologies. Or they may be more general like a belief in freedom or equality. Or they may be habits of mind, attitudes and prejudices. Many of them are shaped by our upbringing and education as well as our later experience of life. We each have a web of beliefs, values and attitudes that makes us the people we are and influences, for good or ill, the way we live our lives.

TO DO

Individually or as a group, make a list of as many "isms" as you can think of. Jot down in a sentence what kind of belief each "ism" stands for.

Take 20 minutes for this

In most democratic societies, different belief and value systems are allowed to live side by side. Indeed, democracy is based on its own beliefs and values: people are free to choose their standpoint and the beliefs and values they will live by. This freedom of choice and tolerance of different beliefs is called pluralism. Pluralism means that everyone has the right to choose their own beliefs and values. The implied premise is that all beliefs and values are equal. What this viewpoint cannot allow is that any particular belief might be right and the others wrong. So people are free to worship one God or many gods or no god at all. As far as society is concerned, no position is true or false; it's just a matter of personal opinion.

This is another reason why religious beliefs have been pushed out of public life into private life. As we saw in Session One, facts are easier to handle than beliefs. They have the advantage of being definite and of being seen to be either right or wrong. Beliefs and values cannot be dealt with in the same way; there is no simple way of proving or disproving them. It is easier and more convenient to keep religious beliefs apart from public life: politics and religion must be kept separate. Religion has no significant place in business or public administration, and has only a restricted role in the media and in education. And as the media represent political and economic affairs as the most important things in life, religion appears by its absence unimportant. The important news happens in Parliament and the City, the town hall and the boardroom. Religious belief, far from addressing the most important questions in life, is a minority "leisure" interest.

But beliefs aren't just personal whims: it does matter what beliefs you hold. It makes a difference to people's lives whether you have communism or capitalism. It matters whether you believe that human beings are made in the image and likeness of God or are the products of chance. It matters whether you believe that each person is precious or not. It matters whether you believe life is for getting what you want or for giving. It matters whether you believe that the most important thing is to make the nation great or to feed the world's hungry. Beliefs and values matter, but they are not all equally valid. Christians have something important to say not just for people's private interest, but for the public good.

What is at the heart of Christianity? Jesus summed it up in the commandments to love God with our heart, mind, soul and strength, and to love our neighbour as we love ourselves (Mark 12.30–31). John pointed to it when he wrote that "God loved the world so much that he gave his only Son, so that everyone who believes in him may not die but have eternal life." (John 3.16)

And Paul put his finger on the heart of the Christian message when he wrote these words . . .

BIBLE STUDY

I may be able to speak the languages of men and even of angels, but if I have no love, my speech is no more than a noisy gong or a clanging bell. I may have the gift of inspired preaching; I may have all knowledge and understand all secrets; I may have all the faith needed to move mountains—but if I have no love, I am nothing. I may give away every-

13

thing I have, and even give up my body to be burnt—but if I have no love, this does me no good.

Love is patient and kind; it is not jealous or conceited or proud; love is not ill-mannered or selfish or irritable; love does not keep a record of wrongs; love is not happy with evil, but is happy with the truth. Love never gives up; and its faith, hope, and patience never fail.

Love is eternal. There are inspired messages, but they are temporary; there are gifts of speaking in strange tongues, but they will cease; there is knowledge, but it will pass. For our gifts of knowledge and of inspired messages are only partial; but when what is perfect comes, then what is partial will disappear.

When I was a child, my speech, feelings, and thinking were all those of a child; now that I am a man, I have no more use for childish ways. What we see now is like a dim image in a mirror; then we shall see face to face. What I know now is only partial; then it will be complete —as complete as God's knowledge of me.

Meanwhile these three remain: faith, hope, and love; and the greatest of these is love.

1 Corinthians 13

SOME QUESTIONS

1 Make a list of the main characteristics of love. Opposite each characteristic write down its opposite.

2 Where did Paul get his picture of love from?

3 What would happen if people lived like this?

4 Why is love more important than all the other things Paul mentions?

5 How can people live a life of love?

What would you say ...

...to someone who said that it doesn't matter what you believe as long as you are sincere?

14

SESSION THREE

"Science has made religion redundant"

We live in a scientific age. Scientists have unlocked the secrets of the atom and the gene and have probed the galaxies. Today's schoolchildren know more about the physical universe than all their predecessors put together. In the developed world, people are surrounded by the fruits of scientific enquiry and technological inventiveness. We take television, cars, aircraft and computers for granted and yet all these things have happened in a very short space of time.

Since the battles over Creation and Evolution in the 19th century, the relationship between science and religion has been an uneasy one. There is a widespread feeling that science has somehow disproved religion. People no longer look to God to produce miracles; they look to the scientists. One of the assumptions at the heart of the conflict is that there is only one right explanation of the world. So either the scientific explanation or the religious one must be wrong. Sadly the debate has often focussed on the first two chapters of the book of Genesis. The assumption has been that a thumbs-down here puts the whole Bible in question.

Real life and real religion are more complicated than this yes-or-no, right-or-wrong type of attitude. The people who were inspired to write the Bible thousands of years ago didn't know as much as we know about the physical world. Their picture of how things came to be was, in some ways, much simpler than ours. But the basic questions they were trying to answer—Why is there a universe? Why do we exist? What is human life for?—are just as important today as they were then. The answers that Genesis 1–2 give are just as relevant today as well.

Religion and science needn't be competitors. The truth about the universe is a many-sided thing and each branch of study can complement and add to, rather than take away from, the other. Conflict between science and religion only arises when one side or the other insists that its explanation of reality is the *only* explanation.

TO DO

Read these four statements out.

"Man is nothing but:
Fat enough for seven bars of soap
Iron enough for one medium-sized nail
Sugar enough for seven cups of tea
Lime enough to whitewash one chicken coop
Phosphorous enough to tip 2,200 matches
Magnesium enough for one dose of salts
Potash enough to explode one toy crane
Sulphur enough to rid one dog of fleas."
C E M Joad, as quoted by Andrew
Knowles in Going Firm (Falcon)

"On at least one planet, and perhaps on millions, conditions of temperature, chemical environment, radiation, and the chance congregation of simple atoms, permitted the coming into being of quite elaborate molecules with the power of replicating themselves in that environment. In a remarkable interplay of contingent chance (to get things going) and lawful necessity (to keep things going) there had begun a process by which systems of ever-increasing complexity would evolve. On our planet this eventually led to you and me."
As quoted by J Polkinghorne in The
Way the World Is (Triangle)

16

"We have the paradox of man as the summit of the cosmic development so far, for his mental activities transcend all, yet at the same time he is tragically aware of his personal and social shortcomings and subject to the tension between the awareness of the finitude of his individual life and the infinity of his longings ... Man constitutes a break in the evolutionary process which had hitherto depended on the continuous operation of natural "laws". For man appears to himself to have a free will allowing him to make choices ..."

A Peacocke, **God and the New Biology** *(Dent)*

When I look at the sky, which you have made, at the moon and the stars, which you set in their places— what is man, that you think of him; mere man, that you care for him?

Yet you made him inferior only to yourself; you crowned him with glory and honour.

You appointed him ruler over everything you made; you placed him over all creation: sheep and cattle, and the wild animals too; the birds and the fish and the creatures in the seas.

O LORD, our Lord, your greatness is seen in all the world!

(Psalm 8.3–9)

Compare these statements.

Do they cancel each other out?

Which ones tell you most about yourself and why?

Spend 20 minutes on this

One of the mistakes that believers have often made over the centuries has been to argue that God must be directly responsible for the things they don't understand. In the 18th century, for example, people looked at the marvellous designs of

17

nature which they admired but could not explain, and argued that they proved there was a great designer, namely God. Since that time, many of the things which people then could not explain, except as evidence of God's direct intervention, have been explained by science in more natural ways. Gradually, as the scientists have been able to explain more and more about nature, God has been pushed further and further out of the picture. Today God is no longer needed to explain how bats came to navigate or how the eye is capable of seeing.

But before people push God out of the picture altogether they should consider the implications. If the universe we know is not God's creation, why does it exist at all? If there is no God at the heart of everything then is the whole universe just the result of blind chance. Are we, if you like, the chance end-products of an amazing set of coincidences? If there is no God then there is no ultimate meaning or purpose of life either.

In fact, the picture of an empty universe that has come about by chance does not square with the scientific evidence anyway. The universe is not totally chaotic: there are fixed patterns which science can discern. There is order as well as chaos. People who believe the universe takes its form from random chance and not God's design still have to account for the order and reliability that they see around them.

For Christians, the order and reliability of nature speak of both the faithfulness and loving purposes of a Creator. Christians believe (and the Bible says) that the universe is not here by chance but that it was intended by God. Indeed, we believe that God was not only responsible for the beginning of creation, but that he continues to keep the universe in being through his power, love, and faithfulness to what he has made.

We believe that God not only created and sustains the universe, but he cares so much about his creation that he became deeply and personally involved in its rescue. In the following well known story from Luke's gospel, Jesus declares his manifesto. Here, the God who existed before time or space, came among us in person to reveal his will and purpose. God the creator is also the God who cares for his creatures.

BIBLE STUDY

Jesus returned to Galilee, and the power of the Holy Spirit was with him. The news about him spread throughout all that territory. He taught in the synagogues and was praised by everyone.

Then Jesus went to Nazareth, where he had been brought up, and on the Sabbath he went as usual to the synagogue. He stood up to read the Scriptures and was handed the book of the prophet Isaiah. He unrolled the scroll and found the place where it is written,

"The Spirit of the Lord is upon
 me,
because he has chosen me to
bring good news to the poor.

He has sent me to proclaim
 liberty to the captives
and recovery of sight to the
 blind;
to set free the oppressed
and announce that the time has
 come
when the Lord will save his
 people."

Jesus rolled up the scroll, gave it back to the attendant, and sat down. All the people in the synagogue had their eyes fixed on him, as he said to them, "This passage of scripture has come true today, as you heard it being read."

Luke 4.14–21

SOME QUESTIONS

1 If Jesus speaks with the voice of God, how would you describe God's attitude towards his creation?

2 In what way and through what channels does God care for his creation?

3 What did Jesus come to achieve?

4 What, according to this passage from Luke, are we intended to be?

5   Look at Genesis 1 and Luke 4.14–21. What signs of love, order and purpose can you discover in these stories?

What would you say...

...to someone who says that science has made religion redundant?

SESSION FOUR

"Common sense and goodwill will solve the world's problems"

For many people one of the main functions of religion is to provide moral guidelines. "Leading a 'good' life" and "being a Christian" are often thought to be the same thing. Many parents want to give their children a Christian upbringing mainly because they want to give them a set of moral values.

Other people believe that moral values and religion can be separated. Moral values, they argue, need not be derived from religion. Moral values are more a matter of common sense and goodwill; there is no need to bring God into it.

In practice, working out what common sense is is not as easy as it sounds. As I have said in previous sessions we live in a society where there are many beliefs and value systems. Not surprisingly people with different beliefs approach moral questions from different angles. In the following example what is common sense to one person may be nonsense to someone else.

TO DO

Here are some different points of view about the question of pornography.

Women's rights view
Pornography exploits and debases women

Civil liberties view
All censorship is wrong

Christian view
The body is the temple of the Holy Spirit

Consumer's view
Pornography is a matter of private choice

Publisher's view
Pornography meets a need

1 Divide into small groups, each to discuss a different one of the five viewpoints, and list reasons to support that viewpoint. (10 minutes)

2 Allow 2 minutes for each group to present their case to the other groups. (10 minutes)

(Some group members may find it difficult to represent a viewpoint they don't themselves believe in. In order to learn from the exercise they should try to see the problem from the viewpoint they are presenting, and present it as convincingly as they can. Afterwards they may feel free to dissociate themselves from the viewpoint that they presented in the exercise.)

3 Finally discuss whether there is a common-sense point of view. (10 minutes)

Not only do moral values vary from person to person but they also vary from age to age. In the not-too-distant past, ideas like duty, service and patriotism were very important in people's thinking. Today these virtues are much less prominent. People nowadays place a very high value on personal freedom and personal rights. The anti-communism of the 1950s seems dated in the days of *perestroika* and *glasnost*. The place of women in society has changed. People's attitudes towards authority have changed. Ideas do not stand still and moral values change as well. The notion of morality based on common sense has to contend not only with the differences between people but also with the differences of culture and time.

Differences of culture and time also affect the morality derived from the Bible. Paul lived in an age that took slavery for granted whereas today it is almost universally abhorred. Christians and Jews no longer practise animal sacrifice. These and other changes in religious attitudes and practices remind us that the Bible has to be interpreted with great care. Nevertheless the Word of God offers a timeless and authoritative basis for morality which common sense can hardly match. Christians for centuries have found its message relevant in their lives. In the Bible are the Maker's instructions designed to enable all people to achieve their fullest potential as sons and daughters of God. It provides a yardstick by which to judge the many changes in ideas and attitudes which in turn affect people's moral values and practices. As Jesus himself put it, ". . . anyone who hears these words of mine and obeys them is like a wise man who built his house on rock. The rain poured down, the rivers overflowed, and the wind blew hard against that house. But it did not fall, because it was built on rock." (Matthew 7.24–25)

A much greater problem for those who believe they can base morality on common sense and goodwill is the problem of goodwill. To be more precise, working out what the rules are is only half the battle. Putting the rules into practice is much harder.

TO DO

Make a list of all the people who would be out of a job if people were unfailingly trustworthy, honest, honourable and caring!

Spend 10 minutes on this

23

The idea that a bit more goodwill will solve the human problem really does not take the flawed nature of human beings seriously enough. It ignores the real problem which is the corruptibility of the human heart. Jesus was only too well aware of the real problem about people. He knew that "From the inside, from a person's heart, come the evil ideas which lead him to do immoral things, to rob, kill, commit adultery, be greedy and do all sorts of evil things; deceit, indecency, jealousy, slander, pride and folly." (Mark 7.21–22) The Bible calls this human corruptibility sin, and has a great deal to say about the subject. Above all, Christians believe that Jesus Christ came into the world to deal with human sin. We believe the whole point of the Christian faith is not just to provide people with moral guidelines but also to effect a deep and radical change in people's lives by rooting out sin and replacing it with goodness and love. A change of heart and, through that, a change in the way we live our lives is (or ought to be) the very centre of the Christian experience. It is a change that comes about when people begin to realize how much God loves them. That realization happens when people begin to understand what the cross means, and when they deepen that understanding through reflecting on the scriptures. John brings together many of these ideas in one of his letters.

BIBLE STUDY

Dear friends, let us love one another, because love comes from God. Whoever loves is a child of God and knows God. Whoever does not love does not know God, for God is love. And God showed his love for us by sending his only Son into the world, so that we might have life through him. This is what love is: it is not that we have loved God, but that he loved us and sent his Son to be the means by which our sins are forgiven.

Dear friends, if this is how God loved us, then we should love one another. No one has ever seen God, but if we love one another, God lives in union with us, and his love is made perfect in us.

24

We are sure that we live in union with God and that he lives in union with us, because he has given us his Spirit. And we have seen and tell others that the Father sent his Son to be the Saviour of the world. If anyone declares that Jesus is the Son of God, he lives in union with God and God lives in union with him. And we ourselves know and believe the love which God has for us.

God is love, and whoever lives in love lives in union with God and God lives in union with him. Love is made perfect in us in order that we may have courage on Judgement Day; and we will have it because our life in this world is the same as Christ's. There is no fear in love; perfect love drives out all fear.

So then, love has not been made perfect in anyone who is afraid, because fear has to do with punishment.

We love because God first loved us. If someone says he loves God, but hates his brother, he is a liar. For he cannot love God, whom he has not seen, if he does not love his brother, whom he has seen. The command that Christ has given us is this: whoever loves God must love his brother also.

1 John 4.7–21

SOME QUESTIONS

1 How, according to John, are our hearts changed?

2 What are the signs that God's love dwells in our hearts?

3 What does the cross do for us?

4 What does "love our brother" really mean?

What would you say . . .
. . . to someone who believes that common sense and goodwill will solve the world's problems?

SESSION FIVE

"The pursuit of personal happiness is the main purpose of life"

Modern Western culture has produced a very individualistic kind of society. For many centuries ordinary people's lives were largely bound by the iron laws of tradition and necessity. People generally lived in the same place all their lives, and pursued the occupations that their station in life demanded. There was little personal freedom or personal choice for the majority of people. Education was rudimentary or non-existent for most of the population. Life was hard, and working people were dependent on those who owned the land or those who owned the industries. Social classes sharply divided people from one another, and society was traditional, hierarchical and authoritarian. Personal choice and freedom was limited by one's place in the hierarchy and the sheer poverty which so many people had to endure. Life expectancy was short and infant mortality was high. There was little protection or welfare for the ill or the weak. There was little or no luxury except for the privileged upper classes. Many Third World countries are still like this.

By contrast, modern Western societies based on a belief in personal freedom and equality have transformed the lot of most ordinary people. Legal protection, trade unions and the welfare state have provided a safety net for people. Universal education and changing attitudes have weakened the power of the class system. Affluence has enabled millions to exercise much greater freedom to choose where they will live; how they will earn their living; whom they will marry; what lifestyle they will adopt; and what kind of beliefs and values they will express. In short, personal freedom and equality have produced an individualistic society, where citizens can make of their lives what they like.

TO DO

Try to imagine how life was for most Europeans at the beginning of the 20th century. Each make a list of the things that have changed. Compare your list with those of other members of the group. Are all these changes for the better? Discuss as a group.

Spend 20 minutes on this

The increase in personal freedom in Western societies has raised new questions and created new problems. It has created an enormous market place where countless voices compete to persuade the consumer that their product or service will provide instant happiness. It is a market place full of dreams appealing to people's pride or their desire for power or pleasure. It is a restless place always seeking something new and something different, and dominated as much by fashion as the society of the past was dominated by tradition and necessity. Nothing is supposed to last. Few things stay the same, except a longing for happiness.

In such a restless environment it is hardly surprising that there are new and disturbing social problems. Despite increasing affluence, many Western societies continue to see their crime rates rise. The stability of family life has also suffered with higher and higher divorce rates and more couples avoiding marriage altogether. As pressures increase, and as people seek more stimulants, so drug and other addictions increase. And the gap between the rich world and the poor continues to widen. The personal freedoms of modern Western culture are a mixed blessing. Personal freedom means personal choice, which can either produce thoughtful,

27

caring citizens or self-centred egoists. A society dedicated to the pursuit of personal happiness can turn into a jungle where only the fittest and the fastest survive, unless there is some real understanding of where true happiness can be found.

Jesus Christ spent a great deal of time trying to teach people not to look for happiness in the wrong places. He was certainly no kill-joy trying to persuade people not to enjoy life. (On the contrary, some of his critics accused him of having too much of a good time (Matthew 11.16–19)!) But over and over again he tried to teach people that their deepest longings would only be satisfied by the love which God yearned to give them. He knew that nothing in the market place of human choices could last. He knew that even the deepest human love was vulnerable to the cruel realities of human imperfection and frailty. He constantly urged people to get their priorities right and seek the pearl of great price (Matthew 13.45–46). In the following extract from the Sermon on the Mount, Jesus warns his followers to be very discerning about the choices they make.

BIBLE STUDY

"Do not store up riches for yourselves here on earth, where moths and rust destroy, and robbers break in and steal. Instead, store up riches for yourselves in heaven, where moths and rust cannot destroy, and robbers cannot break in and steal. For your heart will always be where your riches are.

"No one can be a slave of two masters; he will hate one and love the other; he will be loyal to one and despise the other. You cannot serve both God and money.

"This is why I tell you not to be worried about the food and drink you need in order to stay alive, or about clothes for your body. After all, isn't life worth more than food? And isn't the body worth more than clothes? Look at the birds: they do not sow seeds, gather a harvest and put it in barns; yet your Father in heaven takes care of them! Aren't you worth much more than birds? Can any of you live a bit longer by worrying about it?

"And why worry about clothes? Look how the wild flowers grow:

28

they do not work or make clothes for themselves. But I tell you that not even King Solomon with all his wealth had clothes as beautiful as one of these flowers. It is God who clothes the wild grass—grass that is here today and gone tomorrow, burnt up in the oven. Won't he be all the more sure to clothe you? How little faith you have!

"So do not start worrying: 'Where will my food come from? or my drink? or my clothes?' (These are the things the pagans are always concerned about.) Your Father in heaven knows that you need all these things. Instead, be concerned above everything else with the Kingdom of God and with what he requires of you, and he will provide you with all these other things."

Matthew 6.19–21, 24–33

SOME QUESTIONS

1 What are the snags and pitfalls of earthly treasures?

2 What does "treasure in heaven" mean?

3 Do you agree that it is impossible to devote your life to God and to money? Where does your own loyalty lie?

4 Jesus suggests that there is a connection between consumerism and fear and anxiety. Do you think this is true and if it is, why do you think this is so?

5 Do you really believe that God will look after your practical needs?

6 What is God's Kingdom (verse 33) and why is it so important?

7 What, according to Jesus' teaching, is the real purpose of human life?

What would you say . . .
. . . to someone who believed that the pursuit of personal happiness was the main purpose of life?

SESSION SIX

"This life is the only one"

Many people don't give life after death much thought. Some people don't believe in an afterlife at all. From this point of view, life is a journey without any final destination. We live and die and that is the end of us.

Others do have a belief in life after death, but there is nothing particularly religious about their beliefs. The afterlife is seen as an extension of this life. It is centred on people's desires to be reunited with their loved ones. It is a life that is somehow free from earthly pain and sorrows. But it is an idea of life after death that is not based on the Christian understanding of the Kingdom of God.

Christians also believe in life after death. Our vision of this afterlife is centred on God. We base our belief of life after death on the resurrection of Christ. This event indicates that death is not final. Christians believe that Jesus Christ was the first of all those who are to be raised from death. We believe that his resurrection gives good grounds for the belief that we have an eternal destiny.

What people believe about our final destiny should make a lot of difference to their everyday lives. In practice, longer life expectancy probably enables most people to postpone any serious consideration of such ultimate questions.

TO DO

Put the following concerns in order of priority from 1 (top priority) to 10 (lowest priority).

A successful career
Bringing up a family

Making a home
Being a Christian
Creating a happy marriage
Having an interesting social life
Getting to heaven
Making this a better world
A long and healthy life
Interesting hobbies

Spend 10 minutes on this (and be honest!)

Share your order of priorities with the rest of the group.

Did everyone agree about the top three priorities? If not why not?

Where did getting to heaven come in people's lists?

Spend 20 minutes on this

Does belief in life after death really matter? If we are going to have to meet God, the answer must be yes. In his presence, we shall see ourselves as we really are, good and bad. His goodness, love and truth will show up any lack of these qualities in ourselves. If we have to do with God in the next world, then we are in some sense accountable to him for what we have become in this world. The two worlds are connected. If our ultimate destiny is to stand before our Maker, our decisions now will affect our ultimate standing. Jesus made this connection plain when he told the disturbing story of the rich man and Lazarus (Luke 16.19–31).

Central to this connection between this world and the next is our relationship to God. Throughout our earthly lives we have countless opportunities to turn towards God in love, worship and obedience or to turn away from him in unbelief, indifference or sin. If we have spent a lifetime turning away from God we shall hardly want to be with him and enjoy his

31

presence for the rest of eternity. For his part, God will never force his presence on us. In the end, the result of an unrepentant turning away from God can only be the pain of separation from the One who truly loves us. It is not God's will that we should be estranged from him, but in the end he respects our freedom to choose this. But in choosing separation from God we cut ourselves off from the source of all goodness, life and love. Such a choice must ultimately be a dead end. Hence our attitude to life after death is enormously important. If we are designed for eternity with God, then to live this life as if there is no eternal life or no God is a terrible mistake. It is ignoring the destiny for which we were created.

Critics of Christianity argue that the Christian belief in heaven and hell has often been used to frighten people into obedience and make ordinary people put up with intolerable conditions in their earthly lives. Sadly this has often been the case, but it is a distortion of Christianity. Jesus came so that men and women could have life in all its fullness. By that he didn't just mean heaven. Much of his ministry was spent healing the sick and helping people to attain a deeper wholeness in this life, as well as pointing them to eternal realities. A Christianity that diminishes the quality of people's lives is a distortion of the gospel.

Christians' concern with the next life is not just for ourselves. It is the longing that the loving purpose of God should be fulfilled in the homecoming of all his children and the completion of his purpose for all Creation. To those who have begun to glimpse something of God's love for them, the prospect of heaven is a wonderful one. For heaven is really a homecoming—to a home where we are deeply loved, valued and cherished. No wonder Jesus spoke about heaven in terms of banquets and parties. In one of his most famous stories, he describes what happens when a child of God ends up in his Father's arms.

BIBLE STUDY

"There was once a man who had two sons. The younger one said to him, 'Father, give me my share of the property now.' So the man divided his property between his two sons. After a few days the younger son sold his part of the property and left home with the money. He went to a country far away, where he wasted his money in reckless living. He spent everything he had. Then a severe famine spread over that country, and he was left without a thing. So he went to work for one of the citizens of that country, who sent him out to his farm to take care of the pigs. He wished he could fill himself with the bean pods the pigs ate, but no one gave him anything to eat. At last he came to his senses and said, 'All my father's hired workers have more than they can eat, and here I am about to starve! I will get up and go to my father and say, Father, I have sinned against God and against you. I am no longer fit to be called your son; treat me as one of your hired workers.' So he got up and started back to his father.

"He was still a long way from home when his father saw him; his heart was filled with pity, and he ran, threw his arms round his son, and kissed him. 'Father,' the son said, 'I have sinned against God and against you. I am no longer fit to be called your son.' But the father called his servants. 'Hurry!' he said. 'Bring the best robe and put it on him. Put a ring on his finger and shoes on his feet. Then go and get the prize calf and kill it, and let us celebrate with a feast! For this son of mine was dead, but now he is alive; he was lost, but now he has been found.' And so the feasting began.

"In the meantime the elder son was out in the field. On his way back, when he came close to the house, he heard the music and dancing. So he called one of the servants and asked him, 'What's going on?' 'Your brother has come back home,' the servant answered, 'and your father has killed the prize calf, because he got him back safe and sound.'

"The elder brother was so angry that he would not go into the house; so his father came out and begged him to come in. But he answered his father, 'Look, all these years I have worked for you like a slave, and I have never disobeyed your orders. What have you given me? Not even a goat for me to have a feast with my friends! But this son of yours wasted all your property on prostitutes, and when he comes back home, you kill the prize calf for him!' 'My son,' the father answered, 'you are always here with me, and everything I have is yours. But we had to celebrate and be happy, because your brother was dead, but now he is alive; he was lost, but now he has been found.'"

Luke 15.11–32

33

SOME QUESTIONS

1 What would have happened if the son had decided not to go home?

2 How would his father have felt if he had not come back?

3 How do you feel about the way the son treated the father?

4 Would you have taken him back if you had been in the father's shoes?

5 What do you think the son's feelings were when he returned?

6 If heaven means coming home to God, what do you think it will be like?

7 What stopped the older son from joining the party?

8 Do the father's words to the older son tell you anything about your relationship with those who do not want to join the party?

What would you say . . .
. . . to someone who believes that this life is all there is?

FURTHER READING

If you would like to follow up some of the ideas in this booklet, the following books should get you started.

Charles Colson   **Against the Night** Hodder & Stoughton, 1989

A F Holmes   **Contours of a World View** IVP, 1983

C S Lewis   **The Abolition of Man** Fount, 1978

Lesslie Newbigin   **The Other Side of 1984** WCC, 1983

Lesslie Newbigin   **Foolishness to the Greeks** WCC, 1986

Lesslie Newbigin   **The Gospel in a Pluralist Society** WCC, 1989

Arthur Peacock   **God and the New Biology** Dent, 1986

John Polkinghorne   **One World** SPCK, 1986

John Polkinghorne   **Science and Creation** SPCK, 1988

John Polkinghorne   **Science and Providence** SPCK, 1989

Drusilla Scott   **Everyman Revived: The Common Sense of Michael Polanyi** Book Guild, Lewes, 1985

James W Sire   **The Universe Next Door** IVP, 1988

Keith Ward   **The Turn of the Tide** BBC, 1986

You may also be interested in the *Gospel and Our Culture* newsletter which can be obtained from the Revd Dr H D Beeby, c/o The Selly Oak Colleges, Bristol Road, Birmingham B29 6LQ.